PET THAT CAT!

A HANDBOOK FOR MAKING FELINE FRIENDS

by NIGEL KIDD & RACHEL BRAUNIGAN

of *I've Pet That Cat*

QUIRK BOOKS
PHILADELPHIA

Library of Congress Cataloging-in-Publication Data
Names: Kidd, Nigel, author. | Braunigan, Rachel, author.
Title: Pet that cat! : a handbook for making feline friends / by Nigel Kidd & Rachel Braunigan of I've pet that cat.
Description: Philadelphia, PA : Quirk Books, [2022] | Includes bibliographical references. | Audience: Ages 7+ | Summary: "A handbook that teaches kids how to meet, care for, and celebrate cats" —Provided by publisher.
Identifiers: LCCN 2021049062 (print) | LCCN 2021049063 (ebook) | ISBN 9781683693147 (paperback) | ISBN 9781683693154 (ebook)
Subjects: LCSH: Cats—Juvenile literature.
Classification: LCC SF445.7 .K53 2022 (print) | LCC SF445.7 (ebook) | DDC 636.8/083—dc23/eng/20211006
LC record available at https://lccn.loc.gov/2021049062
LC ebook record available at https://lccn.loc.gov/2021049063

ISBN: 978-1-68369-314-7

Printed in China

Typeset in Staring Contest, Ugiftig, Klinic Slab, and Iskra

Designed by Elissa Flanigan
Production management by John J. McGurk

Quirk Books
215 Church Street
Philadelphia, PA 19106
quirkbooks.com

10 9 8 7 6 5 4 3 2 1

Thank you to my cats:
Fred, Cherry, and Princess Cadbury Crème
Kitten. Thank you for being my friends.

Contents

Introduction
I've Pet That Cat!

My name is Nigel, and I love cats! I also love reading. The first book I ever learned to read was a picture book called *Cat Traps*, by Molly Coxe. My brother taught me to read it because he knew I loved cats. When I got older, I often read to my cats, Kenny and Fred. They'd snuggle on my bed, and we would go on adventures together. Writing this book brings together two of my favorite things!

What I love about cats is that they are all so different: Cats can be cuddly, aloof, feisty, or playful. They can have long hair or short hair, or stripes or swirls in their fur. Some have no fur at all! And every cat has their own unique personality. Learning about cats can help you become a better friend to them.

Getting to know a new cat is like reading a new book. Each has a different story. I hope this book helps you learn more about cats and encourages you to get to know them. Most of all, I hope you make some new feline friends!

How to Pet That Cat

Getting to know a cat takes a little
work, but it's worth it! If you take
your time, you may make a new
feline friend.

When you meet a new cat, you might want to pet them right away. But if you follow a few simple steps, you're more likely to have a successful cat encounter. Before you pet that cat, let's learn how!

1. Ask the Caregiver.

Just like any other pet, it is important to ask the caregiver before you pet a cat. Caregivers know their cats better than anyone else. Some cats may be afraid of new people or may not like being petted. A caregiver can tell you if their cat likes to meet new people and give you tips on how to approach their cat.

If the caregiver says no, that's okay! A good friend always respects boundaries. Saying thank-you and walking away shows that you respect the caregiver and their cat.

2. Ask the Cat, Too.

Now that the caregiver has said yes, it is time to ask the cat. Research shows that cats have better and longer interactions with people who let cats initiate contact. Rushing up to pet a cat may just make her run and hide. If you sit quietly and wait for the cat to approach you first, she will be less scared. You're also more likely to make a new friend!

3. Introduce Yourself.

When you and your feline friend-to-be are ready, it's time to introduce yourself! First make your body smaller by getting down to the cat's level, and slowly put your hand out. Give

the cat a chance to approach and smell you on his own. If he doesn't, you can slowly reach forward and let him smell your hand. After a few seconds, try gently stroking him on the cheek.

It's important to watch how the cat responds before touching him again. If he comes closer, or rubs against you, he is saying you can pet him. If he backs away, hisses, flattens his ears, or tries to swat at you, it's best to stand up and walk away.

4. Pet That Cat!

Cats like to have their fur petted in the direction it grows. That means petting from the head toward the tail. If you pet

a cat from their tail to their head, this rubs the fur in the wrong direction. Most cats dislike this feeling.

Respecting how a cat wants to be petted is important. If you take their feelings into account, a cat is more likely to become your friend.

Cats will often tell you when they have had enough petting. They may walk away, thump their tail, or even gently nip your hand. If this happens, it's okay. When a cat does this, they are saying they no longer want to be touched. Respect their wishes and let them be. Part of becoming better friends with a cat is showing that you know when to leave them alone!

Tips from Nigel

Knowing when to stop petting a cat is just as important as getting the cat's permission to pet him. Pay attention to what a cat is telling you with their body language (see page 19 for more).

Where to Pet a Cat (and Where Not To!)

When you first meet a cat, the first place you should pet is behind the ears or on the cheek. Most cats like to be petted in these places. If the cat responds happily, you can move to petting the top of their head or the middle of their back.

Many cats dislike being petted on their tail, the base of their tail, their belly, or their paws. Even if a cat rolls happily onto his back, think carefully before petting that belly. It's often a trap! A cat's belly is sensitive, and most cats don't like that area of their body being touched. Getting to know a cat will help you learn where they want you to pet them and where you should avoid.

Picking Up a Cat

Picking up a cat can be risky if you don't know how to do it safely. Many cats do not like to be picked up.

To pick up a cat safely, make sure to approach them calmly. Place one hand under the cat's upper chest by reaching behind the front legs. While you lift the cat's chest, use your other hand to scoop up the back legs and bottom. Cats like to feel secure, so hold the cat against your body while you lift them. Make sure the cat's bottom is supported and their legs are not loose or dangling. If cats feel like they're in danger, they may scratch you.

If this is your first time picking up or holding a cat, practice this while sitting on the ground, and lift them onto your lap. This is a great way to see if a cat is comfortable with you holding them without the possibility of dropping them.

Although many cats dislike being picked up, some cats like to be held. These cats often enjoy hanging out on your shoulders and watching the world go by.

SUPPORT
CHEST

SUPPORT
BOTTOM

SUPPORT
BOTTOM

SUPPORT
CHEST
(+ FRONT
PAWS)

DOs and DON'Ts

for meeting cats

✔

DO be calm and gentle.

DO try to let a cat approach you first.

DO pet a cat's fur from head to tail.

DO watch the cat for signs that they are done interacting.

DO respect a cat's decision to end the interaction and walk away.

Ø

DON'T pet a cat without first asking permission from the caregiver and the cat.

DON'T pull on a cat's tail.

DON'T pet a cat's belly.

DON'T pet a cat who is hissing or growling.

DON'T pick up a cat you don't know.

These are just a few tips on how to safely get to know a cat. Now that we know the basics, keep reading to learn even more about how to understand cats!

What's That Cat Telling You?

Cats might sometimes seem aloof and mysterious . . . but that doesn't have to be the case! Just like any other pet, cats have their own way of communicating. Understanding their sounds and body language is key to understanding (and befriending) cats. Want to know what cats are saying? Read on.

Cat Body Language

If you pay attention, a cat's body language will tell you everything you need to know. When you understand and respect what a cat is telling you, that cat will grow to trust you more. Here's what to watch for.

The Tail

Cats use their tails for balance. When humans try to keep our balance, we stretch our arms out and try to keep our body centered so we don't fall over. Cats do this with their tails. Their tails are also used for communication. Watching a cat's tail can tell you a lot about his mood.

- If the tail has a **CURVE AT THE TOP** like a small question mark, this is a sign of playfulness. It is okay to pet him or see if he wants to play.

- If the tail is **LOW OR FLAT TO THE GROUND**, this may mean he is feeling nervous, scared, or aggressive.
- If the tail is **COMPLETELY TUCKED UNDER** the cat's body, he is very scared and feels threatened. Give the cat space and don't try to pet him.

- When a cat's tail is PUFFED UP and his back is arched, he is trying to make himself look bigger for a potential fight. The cat is scared and agitated, and he may lash out. Do not pet!

The position of a cat's tail is not the only thing to watch. How a cat moves his tail can also tell you how he is feeling. For example, when a cat is lying close to the ground and his tail is making sweeping motions, this means he is watching something closely. You may see a cat do this while watching birds through a window.

If you are petting a cat and he is flicking his tail from side to side or thumping it on the floor, this is a sign that he is becoming upset. He's saying he's done with petting and he'd like to be left alone now, please. **WARNING:** If you don't obey this request, you might get scratched!

The Ears

A cat's ears can also tell you about their mood. A happy or curious cat's ears will be upright and facing forward. If a cat's ears are sideways or askew, it means they are nervous or unsure of something. If their ears are flattened toward their back, they are feeling defensive and scared. Unless the ears are facing forward or upright, it might not be a good time to pet that cat.

The Eyes

Watch a cat's body language to understand what their gaze is saying. If a cat is staring at you but they seem relaxed, they may just want your attention. But if a cat is staring at you and looks tense, with their ears slanted or to the side, it may mean they feel threatened.

When meeting a new cat, you may feel like staring into their eyes, but don't do it! Cats use an intense stare to assert their dominance over other cats. If you stare intensely at a cat you just met, they might think you are a threat.

Instead of staring, researchers say to try a slow blink. Narrow your eyes while looking at the cat, and slowly blink a few times. Cats see this as an expression of affection. One study showed that when people slowly blinked at a cat they did not know, the cat was more likely to approach them.

Feline Fact!

Every cat has a unique noseprint.

Cat Sounds

Cats don't normally make as much noise as some other pets. They don't bark like dogs or chirp loudly like birds. But they do make many noises beyond the traditional meow. Each of these sounds serves a different function.

Meows

Kittens and their mothers use meowing to communicate; adult cats rarely meow to each other. Scientists believe that cats meow to humans because they want something, and because humans respond to this sound. Feral cats meow much less than domestic cats. Cats may meow because they want food or attention, to play, or to request something, such as to go outside or to have a window opened.

Many cat caregivers can tell you their cats have different meows for different requests—just as a parent knows their baby's different cries for when they are hungry and when they want to be held.

According to Professor Bjarne O. Braastad at the Norwegian University of Life Sciences, a cat makes a chirping "merr" sound when she is happily greeting a caregiver or saying she likes someone. When a meow is elongated, with an "ah" sound stretched out in the middle, a cat wants something. The meows become longer and the "ah" sound more pronounced when the cat doesn't get what she wants!

Listen to the sounds your cat makes and see if you can tell the difference between "I'm hungry!" and "pet me!"

Purring

Purring is the ultimate sign of a happy cat. Although some big cat species do not purr, cheetahs and mountain lions do. Kittens begin purring within a few days of birth—they purr while they nurse!

Most purring seems to occur when a cat is content or happy. Cats often purr when you pet them or when they are falling asleep near you. Researchers have found there are other forms of purring, too. For example, when a cat is hungry or wants something, they may use a special kind of purr. These purrs often have a higher pitch than the typical low, rumbling purr.

Sometimes cats purr when they are frightened, stressed, or ill. Some scientists believe this purring may even have healing properties. There is still a lot people don't know about purring, but it is believed that the sound frequency of purring helps heal a cat's muscles and bones while using very little energy. Some scientists are studying this purring in the hope that it can be used to help astronauts who experience bone density loss while in space.

Chirping

If you've ever seen a cat watch birds or squirrels, you've probably heard them make this distinctive noise, which can also sound like chattering. Both domestic and wild cats chirp. It is thought that cats make this noise when they are hunting and are frustrated that they can't catch their prey. This explains why you're most likely to hear a cat making this noise as they look out a window at the bird feeder.

Hissing

When a cat hisses, she opens her mouth wide, showing her teeth, and lets out a threatening, breathy sound. Her tail is most likely puffed up. She might also arch her back and flatten her ears. This hiss is a warning that the cat feels threatened and may attack to defend herself against the threat. When a cat is hissing, it's time to back off and give her space. Cats often hiss at dogs, unfamiliar cats, or anything else they believe is a threat.

Caterwauling

A caterwaul is a loud, drawn-out yowl. Cats caterwaul to find a mate. A cat will caterwaul less after being spayed or neutered—another reason to get your cat spayed or neutered!

Some cats will make this noise when they see a threat outside the window, such as another cat or animal. And you may also hear it if a cat is hurt or in distress. Caterwauling could be a sign that your cat is in trouble and needs your help, so you should never ignore this sound when you hear it.

Cat Behavior

As anyone who watches cat videos knows, cats do many silly things. Understanding why a cat does the things he does can help you get to know him better.

Feline Fact!

Catnip is not addictive and does not harm cats. Only 70 percent to 80 percent of cats respond to catnip.

Biscuit Making

When a cat uses his front paws to knead a soft surface such as a blanket, pillow, or sometimes even you, we call that **BISCUIT MAKING**. Some people think cats do this because it's the same motion that kittens make to help release milk from their mothers when they are nursing. Another theory is that this behavior is from before cats were domesticated, when they needed to pat down the grass or ground to sleep. Other people think biscuit making may just be a way for cats to spread their scent around and mark objects.

No matter what the reason, when you see a cat making biscuits, you can be sure he is happy and content.

Knocking Things off the Table

Cats are notorious for knocking or pushing our stuff off tables, shelves, and the kitchen counter. Sometimes, cats do this intentionally to get our attention. Other times, they may be trying to play. Just like they bat around a toy mouse (or real mouse), they might want to bat around your computer mouse!

Cats don't always knock things over on purpose. They like to climb and explore. If your bookshelf has knickknacks that are in your cat's path, they might get knocked down. Cats are naturally curious creatures. Instead of getting mad at your cat for these accidents, just clear the shelf.

Bunting

You've probably seen a cat rubbing her chin and cheek against the couch, a table leg, or even your hand. This behavior is known as BUNTING. Cats have scent glands around their chin and cheeks, and bunting leaves their scent behind. Cats use this as a way of saying "I was here!" or marking an object as their own.

Cats also use bunting to show affection. When a cat rubs her chin or cheek against you, she's expressing love and happiness. If you meet a cat for the first time and she does this, it's a sure sign you've made a friend!

If I Fits, I Sits

Cats love boxes. If they fit, they'll sit! But why? Well, cats like small, cozy spaces where they can feel safe. Boxes make them feel secure and comfortable. Studies show that cats with their own boxes or small spaces to hide in are less stressed. Whether it's a cat bed or a box you saved from the recycling, cats enjoy having a cozy spot of their own.

Feline Fact!

Cats only have a few hundred taste buds. (Humans have over nine thousand taste buds.) They make up for this with their sense of smell.

Where's That Cat?

You can find cats in many different places! If you don't have a cat of your own at home, you might know a friend or neighbor who has one. You may even find cats at your local coffee shop or bookstore.

Some local shelters have programs where kids can read to shelter pets. I got to do this once, and it was so much fun! I brought my favorite book, then sat down in a big room filled with cats and read out loud to them. Some cats crawled into my lap, and others rubbed against me. The cats loved the attention.

There are times when you may spot a cat but it's not a good idea to approach them, like when a cat is at the vet or when you meet a stray cat. Some stray cats are friendly, but not all stray cats want to or should be petted. If you find a cat outside that you've never seen before, it's best to let an adult know. They can decide if the cat needs help.

If you keep an eye out, you never know where you might spot a cat!

Meet That Cat!

COFFEE SHOP/
CAT CAFÉ

ON A
PARK BENCH

iN YOUR HOME

iN THE WINDOW OF A FRIEND'S
OR NEiGHBOR'S HOUSE

ON A FARM

LIBRARY/
BOOKSTORE

VETERINARIAN'S
OFFICE / HOSPITAL

LOCAL HUMANE SOCIETY/
CAT SHELTER

BODEGA

Cats Throughout History

Learning all about the history of
cats will help you understand
them better!

Cats have been around for a very long time. They started out as wild animals and were eventually domesticated. Now they're our pets, our friends, and our family members.

A Brief History of Cats

From fossils of the first known cat to the present-day cats we know and love, there is so much to learn about the history of cats.

Proailurus, the First Known Cat

Proailurus means "first cat." We know from fossils discovered in France that this cat lived about twenty-five million years ago. Scientists believe *Proailurus* was a little bigger than the modern housecat, weighed about twenty pounds, and looked similar to a civet. Like modern cats, *Proailurus* had retractable claws that it used for climbing.

Early Domestication

Cats were first tamed over twelve thousand years ago in the area of the world we now call the Middle East. Fossils found on the island of Cyprus tell us that cats were purposely brought there and were most likely already domesticated. Burial sites where the cats were found had been decorated with shells, which indicates that the cats were important to humans. This discovery led to further studies proving the domestication of cats on the mainland surrounding Cyprus many years earlier.

Why were cats domesticated? Domestication of cats was helpful to humans. When people started farming, they also had to store their harvest, but this led to mice eating their grains and endangering the food supply. (The house mouse is a type of rodent that evolved to live near humans and feed off their stores of food!) Wild cats were drawn to farms because of the mice, and humans quickly realized cats could help protect their food from rodents. This was the start of a mutually beneficial relationship.

Cats became so crucial to the protection of food that they were even brought on sea voyages. Rodents were a major problem on ships; they ate the food and damaged ropes and wood. Fortunately, ship cats solved that problem. As ships sailed the seas, cat populations spread throughout the world.

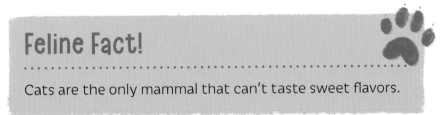

Feline Fact!

Cats are the only mammal that can't taste sweet flavors.

Cats in Ancient Egypt

Cats were often depicted in drawings or carvings in ancient Egypt. Some paintings even showed cats in baskets or sitting on humans' laps, suggesting that these animals were probably pets. Cats were helpful in protecting fields and stored food, as well as guarding against venomous snakes.

Ancient Egyptians believed that cats had many of the same qualities that their gods possessed. Cats were seen as an animal form of certain gods and were revered. When your cat died, the custom was to shave your eyebrows to show you were mourning, a period that lasted until your eyebrows grew back.

The Egyptian goddess Bastet, or Bast, was sometimes depicted as a cat. She was the daughter of the sun god, Ra. The ancient Egyptians believed Bastet rode through

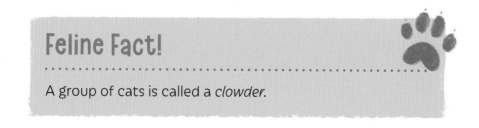

Feline Fact!

A group of cats is called a *clowder*.

the sky with her father during the day, watching over him, and at night she turned into a cat who protected her father from the serpent god, Apep. Worshippers dedicated the mummified remains of their cats to Bastet and even left small carved cat sculptures to honor her.

From the Middle Ages to the Modern Housecat

Cats weren't always as cherished as they were in ancient Egypt. In the Middle Ages, cats were associated with witchcraft. Around 1232, Pope Gregory IX issued a decree proclaiming that black cats were evil. He even encouraged killing cats! Because of this decree, people continued to believe cats were associated with the devil until the 1700s.

It wasn't until the nineteenth century that animal welfare organizations, such as the American Society for the Prevention of Cruelty to Animals (ASPCA), were founded. The founder of the ASPCA, Henry Bergh, fought for legislation to protect animals from abuse.

In 1871, the first large-scale cat show was held in London. The Crystal Palace Cat Show exhibited many breeds, such as Persian cats, Manx cats, and even a Scottish wildcat. More than twenty thousand people attended!

Up until the mid-1900s most cats continued to be outdoor pets. President Calvin Coolidge had many cats in the White House, including the adventurous Tiger. Tiger disappeared once during a snowstorm. President Coolidge was so upset, he had the local radio stations broadcast about his cat. By the next day, Tiger had been located at a navy building about a half mile away. He had sought safety from the storm and stayed when the workers in the building fed him. To keep him safe in the future, Coolidge

got him a collar that read: "My name is Tiger. I live at 1600 Pennsylvania Ave."

The Revolution of Kitty Litter

Before 1947, most people who had cats as pets let them outside to go to the bathroom. Cats that were kept indoors would go to the bathroom in boxes filled with sand, ash, or even soil. These boxes did little to contain the stinky odors and often resulted in a mess.

In 1947, a man named Edward Lowe was working for a company that provided sawdust to factories to soak up spills. Because sawdust was a fire hazard, he tried out a form of granulated clay as an alternative. When his neighbor asked for some sawdust for her litter box, Lowe suggested she use granulated clay instead. His neighbor

Feline Fact!

The oldest cat ever was Crème Puff, who lived to be thirty-eight years old.

was so pleased, she returned a few days later looking for more. Not only was the clay absorbent, but it also helped eliminate odors. He called the new product Kitty Litter.

With this invention, cats could live inside and go to the bathroom without odor or mess. Cat litter completely changed the lives of domestic cats, and they became popular indoor pets. Today there are over three hundred million pet cats in the world!

Myths about Cats

There are many myths about cats, but science, experience, and plain common sense have helped us debunk them.

MYTH: Cats don't become attached to their caregivers.

. . . .

FALSE! When we come home, our dogs run to us and shower us with affection. Cats, on the other hand, show their love in less obvious ways. They may rub against our legs, nap nearby, or quietly purr. While cats are more independent and express their affection more subtly, that doesn't mean they don't love us!

Present Day: Cats with Jobs

Not all household cats are just pets. Some cats have very important jobs, too!

Emotional Support Animals

Emotional support animals (ESAs) are pets who provide comfort to humans and help ease anxiety, depression, or mental health crises. Having a pet has been shown to reduce stress and blood pressure. For an animal to be legally recognized as an ESA, you must have a prescription from a licensed mental health professional.

ESAs are considered assistance animals and allowed to go places where pets cannot, like places with pet restrictions. However, they are not the same as service animals. On airline flights, for example, they are treated like regular pets and don't receive special accommodations.

Cats make great emotional support animals. Their purring is soothing, and they are fairly independent and often happy just to be with you.

Therapy Cats

Whereas emotional support cats help their individual caregivers, therapy cats help groups of people. Therapy cats and their caregivers visit places like hospitals, nursing homes, libraries, and schools. They lie on people's laps or let people pet them to help improve people's moods.

Not just any cat can be a therapy cat. A good therapy cat is calm, travels well, and is comfortable with a variety of people. Therapy cats must be certified from a registered

therapy pet program. This organization meets with the caregiver and the cat to determine if the cat would make a good therapy pet. Usually, the cat and the caregiver receive training. This includes teaching a cat how to be comfortable wearing a harness or leash, visiting different places to assess the cat's comfort level, and training the cat to stay on laps.

Working Cats

Some cats will never be cuddly housecats, or even tame ones. Feral cats who are afraid of people might not be comfortable living in a traditional home. To give these cats a home, some shelters have created working cat programs.

In these programs, feral cats and other outdoor cats can be adopted by businesses to work as natural hunters. Working cats help keep farms, breweries, and warehouses free of rodents while they receive shelter, food, water, and care in return—kind of like early cat-human relationships (see page 40).

Famous Felines

Most of us know famous cats on social media who wear sweaters, go on adventures, and capture our hearts. The following famous felines are known for their heroic acts, their contributions to history, or their unique jobs!

Hemingway's Cats

Ernest Hemingway was a famous writer who lived from 1899 to 1961. He wrote poems, short stories, and novels, including *The Sun Also Rises* and *The Old Man and the Sea*. While Hemingway was living in Florida, a ship's captain gave Hemingway a white, six-toed cat named Snow White. Cats with extra toes are known as POLYDACTYL cats and were considered good luck by sailors. Snow White lived on Hemingway's estate and bore kittens. Those cats multiplied, and at one point over eighty cats lived on his property!

Shortly after Hemingway's death, his home became a museum to commemorate his life. Today the museum staff takes care of the cats who live on the grounds. There are approximately forty cats there at a time, and almost half are polydactyl, like Snow White.

Hemingway liked to name his cats after famous people, and the museum staff continues that tradition. Recent names have included Amelia Earhart, Babe Ruth, and Hercules. What famous person would you name a cat after?

Feline Fact!

Cats have five toes on each front paw and four on each back paw, making a total of eighteen toes. When cats are polydactyl, it is most common for them to have extra toes only on their front paws. It is rare to find a cat who has extra toes on all four paws!

Tabby and Dixie

Abraham Lincoln was the first president to have cats in the White House. Lincoln was a well-known cat lover. When First Lady Mary Todd Lincoln was asked if her husband had any hobbies, she responded: "cats."

Secretary of State William Seward gave Lincoln two kittens. The president named them Tabby and Dixie. The president loved the cats so much, he spoiled them and even had conversations with them! President Lincoln reportedly said, "Dixie is smarter than my whole cabinet. And furthermore, she doesn't talk back."

The president once fed Tabby from a fork during a formal dinner. His response to critics was, "If the gold fork was good enough for former President James Buchanan, I think it is good enough for Tabby."

Feline Fact!

Most orange tabby cats are male. Only about one in five is female.

Chief Mouser to the Cabinet Office

The Prime Minister of the United Kingdom has their own Chief Mouser in their home at No. 10 Downing Street. The first recorded mouser was Peter, who served in 1929. Two more Peters and a female cat named Peta came next. A tabby cat named Larry has held the official title of Chief Mouser to the Cabinet Office since 2011. He was adopted from a shelter by the then prime minister, David Cameron, after the prime minister saw rats near his home.

After Larry was adopted, he took some time to adapt to his responsibilities. It was a few months before he caught his first mouse. There is still some debate over how well he does his job. However, everyone agrees he is an expert napper.

When Larry is not on the prowl for mice, he greets guests who visit the prime minister.

The Algonquin Cat

Since its opening in 1902, the Algonquin Hotel is one of the oldest running hotels in New York City. Besides its long history, it has another unique feature: a resident cat!

In the 1920s, a stray orange tabby found his way into the hotel. The cat was allowed to stay, and the staff named him Rusty. The actor John Barrymore, who was known for his portrayal of Hamlet on Broadway, was a guest at the hotel. He decided the cat needed a more dignified name, and the cat was renamed Hamlet in Barrymore's honor.

Since then, the hotel has had multiple cats. Male cats are given the name Hamlet, whereas female cats are named Matilda. As of this writing, there have been eight Hamlets and three Matildas. The cats are always rescue cats who need a home.

The current Algonquin cat is another orange tabby named Hamlet. He is so popular that people make reservations at the hotel just to see him. The Algonquin employs a Chief Cat Officer to care for Hamlet full-time and manage his fan mail from all over the world. His duties include greeting the guests, sitting at the front desk, and napping. He is very good at napping.

Tama the Stationmaster

Tama was a calico kitten who lived outside the Kishi railway station in Japan. She loved greeting the passengers. People began jokingly calling her the stationmaster.

In 2007, the railway made plans to shut down the train line to Kishi Station to save money, but the local residents urged the railway president to come and meet Tama. The

president loved Tama so much that he ordered a custom hat for her and gave her the formal title of Stationmaster of the Kishi Station. Tama was even given her own ticket booth "office" where visitors could greet her. The number of riders increased, and Tama saved the railway!

In 2009, the railway introduced a redesigned "Tama train." Whiskers were painted on the front of the train, and the station began playing a recording of Tama purring over the public announcement system each time the train stopped.

Tama died in 2015, but her memory lives on. The railway continues to have cat stationmasters named Tama Two, Tama Three, and Tama Four.

Scarlett the Hero Cat

In March 1996, firefighters were called to an abandoned garage in Brooklyn, New York, to put out a fire. Firefighter David Giannelli loved animals and was trained in animal rescue. He heard quiet mews and found three tiny kittens lined up by a brick wall. He whisked them to safety, only to hear more mews a few minutes later. He found two more kittens next to the wall. He realized that the mother cat had been bringing them out of the garage one by one.

David found the mother nearby. The young calico cat was burned and badly injured. The firefighter rushed her and her kittens to the North Shore Animal League for treatment.

The heroic mother cat, who was named Scarlett by the shelter, became a media sensation. Thousands of people wrote letters offering to adopt her and the kittens. Karen Wellen was one of them; she wrote a letter saying she wanted to adopt an animal with special needs because a recent car accident had changed her life. Wellen was chosen as Scarlett's adoptive caregiver.

Scarlett lived a peaceful, quiet life and passed away in 2008. In this brave calico's memory, the North Shore Animal League honors animals who commit heroic acts with the Scarlett Award.

Stubbs, the Cat Mayor of Talkeetna

Stubbs was an orange tabby with a short tail. In 1997, he was found in a cardboard box outside Nagley's General Store in Talkeetna, Alaska. The store's owners adopted him and Stubbs became known throughout the town as the kitten from the store. He would often wander the town and he made friends easily.

That year, he was elected mayor of Talkeetna via a write-in campaign. Talkeetna is a historical district, not a town, so the title of mayor was purely honorary.

People in Talkeetna said they voted for Stubbs because he was honest and he would never raise their taxes. Their only complaint was that he often slept on the job. People came to Nagley's General Store to see Stubbs and called the store his office. Upon entering the store, they often asked, "Where's the mayor?" or announced, "I have an appointment with the mayor."

Stubbs held his post until his death in 2017. Today, the mayor of Talkeetna is Denali, a longhaired cat who also calls Nagley's General Store his office.

MYTH: Black cats are bad luck.

FALSE! One common myth is that black cats cause bad luck. During medieval times in Europe, people believed that the devil appeared as a black cat and that if one crossed your path, it was a bad omen. Now we know that these superstitions aren't true, but black cats continue to be associated with Halloween and witchcraft.

Because of this, black cats are sometimes overlooked in shelters. Don't make this mistake! Black cats make wonderful pets. I have a black cat named Cherry. She can be cranky sometimes, but she is definitely not a witch.

How to Care for a Cat

Now that you know all about
cats and their history, it's time
to learn how to care for them!

Whether you're thinking about getting your own cat, already have a cat, or just like cats a lot, it's important to know how to take good care of them. The more you know, the happier and healthier your feline friend will be.

Adopting a Cat

Shelters take in millions of stray, abused, or abandoned animals each year. They are filled with wonderful, loving pets who just need a wonderful, loving home. Adopting a cat from a shelter or rescue, along with making sure they are spayed or neutered, is one of the best things you can do to help cats.

Shelters have visiting hours when you can meet their cats and get to know them. Most rescue or shelter cats have already been spayed or neutered and are up-to-date on vaccinations. When you pay an adoption fee for your cat, this money pays for those services and allows the shelter to provide help to more animals.

If you want a purebred cat, check for rescue groups in your area who help purebred cats. If you choose to go to a breeder, finding a reputable one is important. A good breeder will be registered and will have references or reviews from veterinarians who work with them. The Cat Fanciers' Association has an Approved Cattery Program in North America, Europe, and Japan, which can help you find registered breeders. Good breeders are willing to answer your questions and will most likely have questions for you, too. Shelters, rescue groups, and good cat breeders all want their cats to go to good homes.

How Do You Choose a Cat?

Cats make excellent pets. They don't need a large house or a yard, and they don't require a lot of training or daily walks. But while cats are more independent than some other pets, they still require your care and attention. They'll do much better in a home that takes their needs into account.

Before you bring a cat home, spend some time getting to know them. When figuring out what kind of cat is best for you, be sure to consider the following:

- **YOUR PERSONALITY:** Look for a cat whose personality suits your own! Are you looking for a snuggly lap cat or an independent companion?
- **YOUR HOME:** Is your home filled with people and noise or is it quiet? Some cats are very social, and others like to be left alone. Some cats dislike loud noises or are easily scared. Look for a cat that will feel comfortable in your home.

Kittens or Cats?

When choosing a cat, adult cats and senior cats are often overlooked in favor of cute kittens. But grown-up cats may be perfect for you, depending on what you and the cat are looking for.

- **SHOULD I GET A KITTEN?** Kittens stay kittens for six to seven months. They love to chew on things and explore their surroundings. Their tiny, sharp claws make it easy for them to climb everything, from curtains and furniture to your pants leg. (I once had a kitten who climbed the door frame in my bedroom!) This adventurous behavior can lead to them getting hurt. Make sure you have the time and energy to care for your kitten and keep them safe.

- **SHOULD I GET AN ADULT CAT?** Adult cats are calmer than kittens and their personalities have fully developed, so it's easier to know if an adult cat is the right fit for you. It's also easier to tell if they get along with children, dogs, or other pets. In addition, they probably have received their vaccinations, have been neutered or spayed, and are already litter trained. Adult cats make great companions.

- **SHOULD I GET A SENIOR CAT?** Sometimes older cats need a new home, but they're often overlooked in shelters. In addition to having the qualities of adult cats, they can be playful in their own way, and they're great at keeping you company. Many have lived their lives around families and are just looking for a safe, loving place to retire.

Are Two Cats Better than One?

Some people believe that cats don't make social connections with other cats. Research has shown that this isn't true. Although some cats do prefer to be the only cat in the house, others enjoy having a friend. So you may want to think about adopting two cats.

Shelters often have bonded pairs who need a home. These are cats who either lived together previously or became close while at the shelter. Adopting bonded pairs together makes it easier for them to adjust to your home.

It's also a good idea to adopt two cats at once when they are littermates. Kittens who know each other prior to adoption tend to get along. Sibling kittens can learn from each other and play together. Also, when kittens have a friend to play with, they cause less mischief.

You can also adopt two cats who aren't bonded pairs or littermates, but you need to consider their personalities. For example, a shy cat might not do well with an outgoing, dominant cat. And before introducing the two cats, they should quarantine from each other for two weeks to make sure they are healthy and have no parasites.

Tips from Nigel

When introducing two cats to each other, do it very gradually! Expose each cat to the other's smell with a toy or something else with the other cat's scent on it. Next, allow the cats to see each other but not interact. If they seem relaxed, you can let them meet. But you should supervise their first few meetings so they don't fight!

A Cat's Basic Needs

My family found a kitten on the side of the road right before Easter. The kitten ran toward my mom, meowing. We tried to find her caregiver, but couldn't. When we brought her home, we knew we had to keep her away from our other cats. We put her in a room with a cat bed, food, water, and some toys. We took her to the vet and learned she had ear mites, fleas, and ringworm. She was so malnourished that she looked only three months old, but she was actually at least six months old! She couldn't meet our other cats or our dog, Cookie, until she was healthy.

We named her Princess Cadbury Crème Kitten. She is gray and white with a little bit of tan on her ears. Princess is healthy now and growing bigger each day. She loves to climb on me and snuggle when I lie down. She carries around small stuffed animals in her mouth, then tosses them up and pounces on them. I'm so happy we found her.

Before bringing a cat home, make sure you can provide the things your new friend will need, like regular veterinary care, vaccinations, food, toys, and a litter box.

Food
·······

There are so many different types of cat food available. Consider these factors when choosing what to feed your cat:

- **AGE:** The age of your cat determines their nutritional needs. Kittens need specifically formulated kitten food so that they grow healthy and strong. Senior cat food will have ingredients that an older cat may need.
- **WET VERSUS DRY FOOD:** Wet foods contain more water, which means your cat does not have to drink as much to stay healthy. As long as your cat is drinking enough water and does not need wet food for a medical condition, it doesn't really matter which type of food you choose. When looking for cat food, find a quality brand name that works with a veterinary nutritionist or ask your veterinarian for recommendations.
- **TREATS:** Treats should be limited to avoid weight gain. Give your cat treats in moderation and they'll live a longer, healthier life.

Litter

When you bring your cat home, she'll need a litter box. Besides a traditional box, you can get a covered box or a self-cleaning litter box.

You'll also need to choose a form of cat litter. Clay litter is the most popular and one of the least expensive choices. Traditional clay litter is not biodegradable and may not manage odors as well as other litters.

Another option is crystal litter, or silica. Silica creates less dust than other litters and absorbs odors and moisture well. Like clay litter, it is not biodegradable.

Looking for something more environmentally friendly? There are multiple types of biodegradable or plant-based litters, like pellets made out of paper, pine, walnuts, corn, or grass seed.

Feline Fact!

Two different tabbies hold the record for most toes at twenty-eight toes each.

No matter what you choose, the most important thing is to keep the litter box clean. Cats prefer a clean place to do their business. If the area is not clean, they may start going to the bathroom someplace they shouldn't!

Beds

Your cat may choose to sleep on the sofa or on your bed. But having her own bed to curl up in will help her feel at home.

Brushing and Bathing

Cats clean themselves by licking their fur. They self-groom and can keep themselves very clean. The few reasons your cat may need a bath include if she has fleas, if she is a cat

who cannot clean herself, or if she is older and unable to keep her fur from matting. Cats do need regular brushing. Brushing removes dead fur, dead skin, and dandruff. It helps reduce shedding and keeps your cat's fur shiny.

Tips from Nigel

Cats need their teeth brushed just like humans. Regular brushing will help your cat avoid gum disease and tooth pain later in life. Human toothpaste is not good for cats. Instead, look for feline toothpastes with cat-approved flavors like tuna!

Toys

Have you ever seen a cat leap on a toy mouse or pounce on a bit of string? That cat is behaving just like a cat hunting real mice in the wild.

A 1992 study by anthrozoologist John Bradshaw found that cats preferred toys with fur or feathers that resemble mice in size and shape. He determined that cats play more enthusiastically when they're hungry, which suggests that cats may actually believe they are hunting.

Playing is also a form of social behavior. Kittens first learn to play with their littermates. They jump, stalk, sneak, and attack just like they would with prey. When kittens have no littermates nearby, they may try this behavior on you!

Cats are predators, so the act of playing is very important. Playing also helps limit weight gain by keeping cats active and reduces boredom. To keep your cat happy, have a variety of toys on hand. Small mouse-shaped toys, small balls, wand toys, lasers, and catnip-stuffed toys are all tried-and-true options.

Feline Fact!

Cats can jump more than six times their height!

Cat Health

Cats need regular veterinary care to ensure they stay healthy. Whenever you bring a new cat into your home, you should take him to a veterinarian for an exam. Your vet can assess if your cat has fleas or other parasites, check his weight, and determine if he has other medical issues.

Cats also need to be vaccinated. Your vet can vaccinate your cat against rabies, distemper, Bordetella, feline leukemia, and other dangerous illnesses. Some vaccines require yearly booster shots. By making sure your cat is up-to-date on his vaccines, you can help him live a longer, healthier life.

Cats should also be spayed or neutered. Spaying and neutering helps reduce the number of cats that wind up in shelters in need of homes. It is also ultimately better for the animal's health. Studies have shown that spaying or neutering your pet reduces their risk of developing certain types of cancers.

If you ever suspect your cat is ill, an appointment with your veterinarian is your best option. Signs of illness include not drinking or eating, not urinating or defecating, decreased activity, diarrhea, coughing, sneezing, and discharge leaking from your cat's eyes, ears, or nose.

Tips from Nigel

Provide your cat with wide or shallow bowls for eating and drinking. If a cat's whiskers touch the sides of the bowl when they eat and drink, they may develop *whisker fatigue*. This can cause stress and lead them to not drink or eat as much as they should.

Outside versus Inside

Long ago, it was normal for cats to roam the neighborhoods and hunt for their food. Nowadays, it's much more common for domesticated cats to live their entire lives indoors. Studies have shown that indoor cats live longer than outdoor cats. By staying inside, a cat avoids dangers such as being hit by a car, fighting other animals, and being exposed to parasites and diseases. There are many ways for your cat to safely spend time outside:

- A **SCREENED WINDOWSILL OR PORCH** allows your cat to enjoy the sun and safely watch the birds.
- If you want to give your cats more outdoor space, a **CAT PATIO**, or "catio," might be the perfect solution! This is a screened-in, enclosed outdoor space that often attaches to a window or a door.
- Try taking your cat for a walk on a **HARNESS AND LEASH**. It may take practice, but some cats love going on walks and exploring.

Tips from Nigel

If you get your cat a harness and leash, it may take time for your cat to become used to them. Have your cat practice wearing the harness and walking on a leash frequently for short periods of time. Always respect when your cat says she has had enough!

Cats who go outdoors often hunt for food, which can have a negative impact on the songbirds and other wildlife in the area. If you have a cat that spends a lot of time outdoors, consider investing in a bird-safe collar. And to keep your outdoor cat safe, only use a breakaway collar, which has a clasp that releases if tugged or pulled on.

What if I'm Allergic to Cats?

Cat allergies are remarkably common. In fact, they are twice as common as dog allergies. While people usually think cat fur causes allergies, the real culprit is a protein called FEL D 1 that exists in cats' dander and saliva.

There are no truly hypoallergenic cat breeds. Almost all cats shed and produce the Fel d 1 protein. However, if your allergies are mild, you may still be able to have a cat. Some cats, including females and neutered males, produce less Fel d 1. The best cat breeds for someone with mild allergies include:

- Balinese
- Cornish rex
- Javanese
- Russian blue
- Sphynx

Before bringing a new cat home, make sure to spend time with them. This will tell you how the cat affects your allergies. Once your cat is home, frequently grooming them and vacuuming will help with mild allergies.

Fostering a Cat

If you want a cat in your life but can't commit to a lifelong placement, fostering might be for you. Rescues and shelters sometimes send cats to foster homes to help them become more socialized and comfortable with humans before finding their forever home. This also gives the shelter more space for other cats staying there. As a foster parent, you will be helping a pet in need.

Fostering can help you determine if a cat is a good fit for your home. When a cat is adopted by their foster parents, this is called a "foster fail." Don't worry—it might sound like a bad thing, but a foster fail means the cat was such a good fit that he was adopted!

If you love kittens and have some extra time and energy, consider fostering motherless kittens. My family once fostered a litter of five kittens. We had to feed them every two hours. I was able to pet them and hold them so they could get used to people. It may be a lot of work, but fostering kittens is fun and rewarding!

Feral Cats

Feral cats are cats who are fearful of humans and have never been socialized to be a pet.

Since feral cats do not make good pets, some are placed in a working cat program (see page 49 for more). For those that are not, communities often come together to trap, neuter, and release (TNR) these cats.

Training Your Cat

Though most of us don't think of training our cats to sit, roll over, or high-five, cats can be trained to do many of the same tricks dogs learn. Most cats will come when you call their name, or at least recognize that you're calling them. With treats and patience, you can train your cat.

Start small. For example, you can train your cat to follow you while dangling a wand toy. If you want your cat to jump through a hoop, first reward her with a treat or praise for touching the hoop with her nose. Then you can reward her for putting her paw on the hoop, putting her head through the hoop, and finally climbing through the hoop.

The Savitsky cats are a group of nine cats trained by their caregivers, Svitlana and Maryna Savitsky, to perform circus tricks. They have appeared with the Big Apple Circus and on the television show *America's Got Talent*.

MYTH: Cats always land on their feet when they fall.

FALSE! This is a dangerous myth. Though cats do have a natural balance system called a *righting reflex* that allows them to reposition themselves and land on their feet, they don't always succeed. Cats may not have enough time to right themselves in a short fall. Larger falls are even more dangerous—cats may injure themselves or be unable to absorb the shock. Cats should never be dropped from heights, tossed, or allowed to climb out high windows. Your cat's safety is very important!

The cats climb poles, jump through hoops, roll barrels, and even jump over each other!

Feline Fact!

Cats lick their paws to use them to clean their face.

Using a Litter Box

Kittens can quickly learn how to use a litter box. Here are simple tips to make the process even easier:

- Use a small, shallow box with no lid or enclosure. It will be easier for them to get in and out.
- Keep the box close and accessible to the kittens.
- Clean the box once a day.
- Clean spills thoroughly. The smell of urine might lead to your cat having accidents outside the box.
- Place a puppy pad under the box to make it easier to clean up accidents.

If you have multiple cats in your home, you'll need multiple litter boxes. And if your cat is litter trained and begins having accidents outside the box, you might want to take her to the veterinarian to check for health issues.

Scratching

Scratching is natural cat behavior. But that doesn't mean you should let your cat destroy your furniture! To allow your cat to scratch to their heart's content, find a scratching post that your cat likes and will use. Cats like tall, stable objects that won't wobble.

When you introduce a new scratching post, place it near the object you don't want your cat to scratch. Show your cat the post, play with them near it, and reward them with treats when they interact with it. Make the furniture they were scratching more unappealing by covering the furniture with double-sided tape, a sheet of tinfoil, or a fitted bedsheet.

While scratching can be frustrating, declawing is not a humane solution. In fact, many countries, including most of Europe, have banned declawing. The Humane Society of the United States and the ASPCA both strongly oppose it. Declawing means amputating the last bone of a cat's toe. This can lead to pain, infections, long-term health issues, and behavioral problems. Say no to declawing!

Marking Territory

Cats use their scent as a way of leaving messages for other cats. They spread their scent by rubbing, scratching, or urinating. Marking an area with their scent is how they warn other cats to stay away. But although marking with urine may be a natural way cats communicate, we don't want this behavior in our homes.

Your cat may be spraying due to mating behavior, stress, or a health issue. If your cat is healthy and neutered but is still marking his territory, he may be stressed. When your cat is stressed, it is often due to conflicts with another cat. You can help reduce his stress by giving him his own space, including his own litter box and food dish. If the problem continues, speak with your veterinarian.

Cat Fights

Cats are territorial and do not like to share. If your cat goes outside, chances are she will fight with other cats. One solution is to keep your cat indoors.

Sometimes when there are multiple cats in a household, there will be fighting. This is why it's crucial to choose cats that are a good match for each other.

If your cats start fighting, don't let them continue. Clapping loudly is one way to help stop the aggression. Like many other behavior problems, cat aggression can be tamed by giving each cat their own litter box, food dish, and bed.

MYTH: Milk and cream are good for cats.

FALSE! Many people think cats love milk, but the truth is that cats can't easily digest dairy, which can make them sick. Avoid giving a cat milk, cream, or other dairy! Other foods to avoid: grapes, raisins, onions, garlic, and chocolate.

Ask the Expert!

To find out more about cats, I interviewed Erin Mayes, a cat behavior specialist who works for PAWS Chicago, a no-kill shelter and rescue.

What is a cat behavior specialist?

A cat behavior specialist is a person who works with cats and knows a lot about them. Most cat behavior specialists have taken classes to learn about cats, their behaviors, and how to help them overcome different types of challenges through training.

What do you do for PAWS Chicago?

I get to work with almost all of the cats that you see at our Lincoln Park Adoption Center. Sometimes, our cats are afraid of new people and environments, or they have a hard time getting along with cats they don't know. After spending time with these cats, I might recommend a specific type of home or person that they will do best with, or develop a training plan to help them become more comfortable at the shelter and in their new homes. I also offer behavior counseling and training plans to adopters and foster families who have questions and concerns about their cat's behavior.

How many cats does PAWS Chicago help each year?

Last year, PAWS Chicago found homes for over 2,100 cats! Every cat that comes to PAWS Chicago receives a spay/neuter surgery, vaccinations, any medical care they might need for illnesses or injuries, and tons of love. And adoption's not the only way we help cats; every year, thousands of already-adopted or community cats receive spay/neuter surgeries, vaccines, and medical help at our Lurie Spay/Neuter Clinic and outreach center.

When a cat first comes to PAWS Chicago, what is done to evaluate his health and personality?

All of our cats are examined by PAWS Chicago veterinarians when they first come to us. Our vets make sure they are spayed or neutered, microchipped, vaccinated, and healthy before they can be adopted. Then, many of our cats head off to foster homes while they wait to find their families. We learn a lot about each cat's personality while in foster care. For instance, we might discover that a cat doesn't want to share attention with another cat and their perfect home's pet-free. Or we may learn that a cat really, really loves other cats and will be happiest with a cat friend, so we make sure they are adopted into a home with other cats! Every cat is unique and we love getting to see their personalities shine.

What kind of cats find a home the fastest? The slowest?

We all love tiny, fluffy kittens, and our kittens six months or younger tend to get adopted pretty quickly. Senior cats over ten years of age, cats with special medical needs, or cats that need a lot of extra behavior training often take longer to find the right home. At PAWS, we never give up on finding a good home for any of our cats, no matter how long it takes. We recently found a home for a ten-year-old cat named Rudy Rudy who had been with us for over six hundred days!

Why are spaying and neutering important?

Did you know that cats can start having babies when they are only six months old? In fact, one unspayed female cat and her offspring can produce 420,000 kittens in just seven years! Reducing the overall number of cats and dogs through spaying and neutering significantly reduces the number of homeless animals in our communities and shelters. Spaying and neutering also decrease or eliminate the risk of certain types of cancer and increase a cat's overall life expectancy.

What advice do you have for someone who is looking to adopt a cat?

There are a lot of things to consider when adopting a cat or kitten. How much time will you have to socialize and play with the cat? Kittens and young adult cats need lots and lots of playtime and enrichment to help them develop as happy and healthy as possible. Adopting young kittens in pairs often helps with this since they can play with each other, but a mature adult or senior might be a better choice for someone with a busy schedule. Cats who are shy may do better in a quiet household with older kids or teens, while confident cats that crave human attention may do best in a household full of kids who can keep them entertained. When adopting a cat, don't be shy! Ask the rescue for background on the cat or foster reports to review so you can get an idea of their personality.

Tips from Nigel

Consider having your cat microchipped, even if they are an indoor cat. These tiny chips injected under your pet's skin allow them to be scanned and identified as yours if they get lost outside.

What can be done to help a new cat adjust to a home that already has other cats?

Take some time! It's easy to want your cats to be best friends, but introducing cats to each other immediately can leave them feeling stressed and confused.

Always follow the guidelines for a slow and controlled introduction. The amount of time it takes to make sure your new cat fits perfectly into your home will depend on each cat.

What can people do to support their local rescues and shelters?

There are plenty of ways to help! Being an animal lover and reading about how to help animals is a great place to start.

If you've found a local shelter you want to get involved with, ask about their fostering or volunteering opportunities. Volunteering might include getting to hang out with adoptable cats, giving them food or water, or doing behind-the-scenes work like helping clean the pets' rooms (a very important job!). As a foster, your family can temporarily care for sick or injured animals, or animals who just need a break from the shelter. If you already have a pet at home, consider donating some of their old toys. Or, if you don't have a pet, make some DIY toys or drop off old blankets for the pets to snuggle up in.

No matter what you do, even if you think it's small, it can make a big impact on the lives of animals who need your help!

Tips from Nigel

A simple way to tell if a cat is a tabby is to look for the *M*. Almost all tabby cats have an M-shaped marking on their forehead.

Name That Cat!

You've learned so much about cats!
Now let's think about names.

If you had to name a cat right this second, what would you name them? This quiz can give you a few ideas.

Every cat has their own unique personality and look. Finding a name to suit them can be a challenge! Here are the top ten most popular cat names.

For male cats:
Oliver, Leo, Milo, Charlie, Simba

For female cats:
Luna, Bella, Lucy, Kitty, Lily

If you're looking for a cat name that stands out from the crowd, follow the directions on the next page and see what you come up with. I should name my cat Marmalade Jigglebelly the Destroyer!

For your cat's first name,
choose the date you were born:

1. Bootsy
2. Yeti
3. Butterscotch
4. Socks
5. Freckles
6. Whiskers
7. Argyle
8. Bandit
9. Cleocatra
10. Sunny
11. Scratchy
12. Tiger
13. King/Queen
14. Muffin
15. Tacocat
16. Macaroni

17. Waffles
18. Stormy
19. Puddles
20. Yoshi
21. Marmalade
22. Curly
23. Catticus
24. Meatball
25. Emperor/Empress
26. Pumpkin
27. Mittens
28. S'mores
29. Patches
30. Princess/Prince
31. Tiny

For your cat's middle name,
choose the first letter of your first name:

A or B: Fuzzikins

C or D: Hisstopher

E or F: Chompsalot

G or H: McClaws

I or J: Radiclaw

K or L: Furball

M or N: Jigglebelly

O or P: Pouncer

Q or R: Tuft-o-fur

S or T: Fluffytail

U or V: Purrific

W or X: Pawfection

Y or Z: Wigglebutt

Finally, for your cat's last name,
choose the first letter of your last name:

A or B: the Clawful

C or D: of the Night

E or F: Meowington

G or H: the Hunter

I or J: Naps-a-plenty

K or L: the Destroyer

M or N: the Great

O or P: Catzilla

Q or R: Cat Detective

S or T: Cattorney at Law

U or V: the Purr Machine

W or X: of the Jungle

Y or Z: the Brave

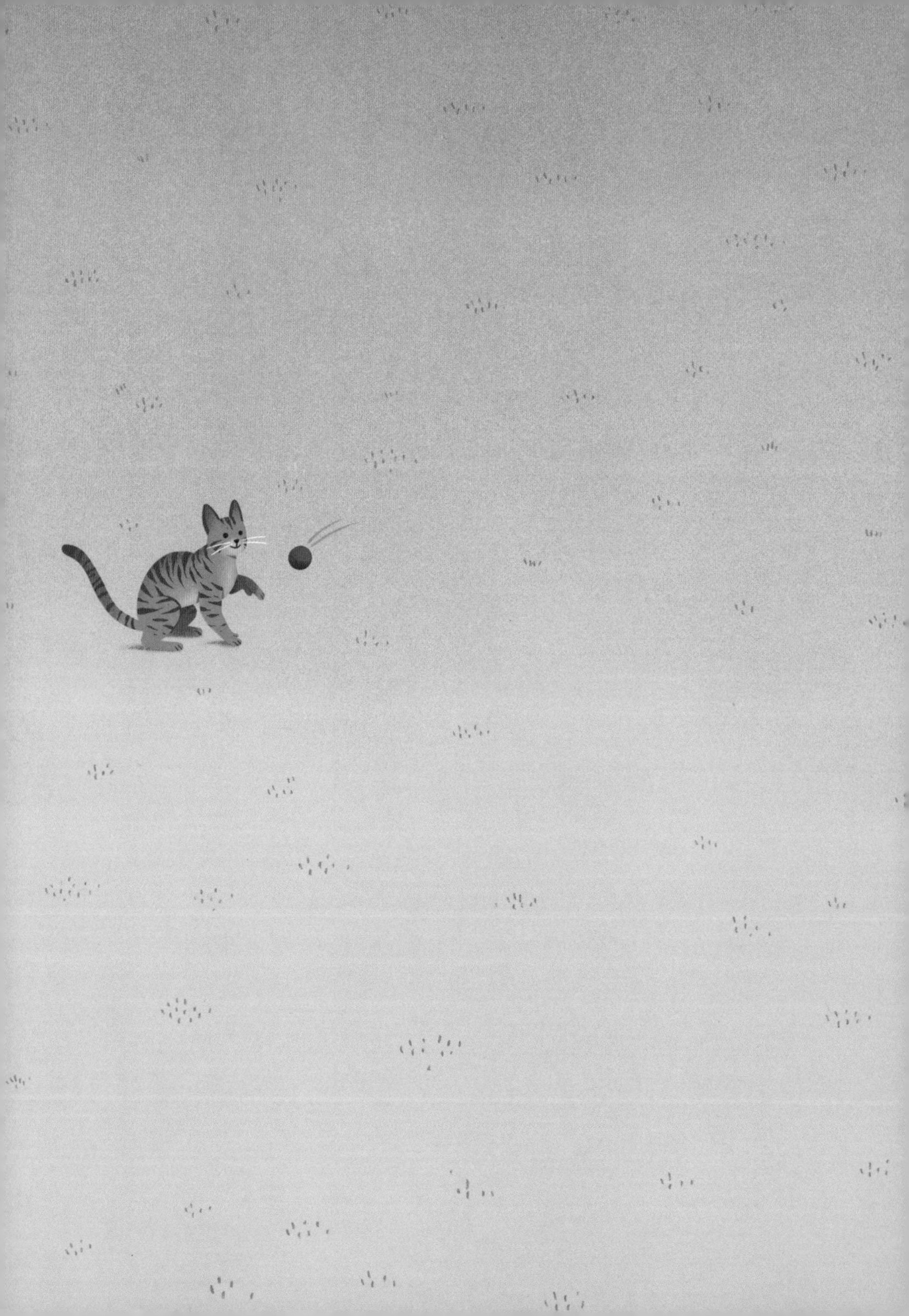

What Is Your Cat Personality?

If you were a cat, what
type would you be?

If you've ever met a cat, you know they're chock-full of cattitude and personality. Want to know what you'd be like as a cat? Take this quiz and discover your cat personality!

1. It's dinnertime! Where would you like to go to eat?

A. Someplace nice and quiet.

B. Nowhere! I'd rather stay home.

C. An all-you-can-eat buffet. Let's chow down!

D. Somewhere I've never been before. Surprise me!

E. The trendy new place that just opened.

F. Pizza, pizza, pizza!

2. What are you going to watch on TV tonight?

A. An old favorite, something I've watched hundreds of times before.

B. Lights out! I want to watch a spooky, scary horror movie.

C. A bake-off, a cook-off, anything with food! I have great taste.

D. Something exciting, like an action movie.

E. Gimme some reality TV. I want drama!

F. You can't go wrong with cartoons.

3. Where would you like to go on vacation?

A. Anywhere, as long as it's with family.

B. Someplace far, far away from other people.

C. A city famous for its mouthwatering cuisine.

D. The mountains. Somewhere I can camp, hike, and climb.

E. A luxurious beach resort. I take my vacations seriously.

F. An amusement park. Let's hit all the roller coasters!

4. Choose a hobby.

A. Knitting

B. Complaining

C. Baking

D. Hiking

E. Photography

F. Video gaming

5. What is your biggest fault?

A. I hate being alone. Come hang out with me!

B. I'm easily annoyed. Just leave me be!

C. I can get a little impatient. Hurry up!

D. I can be a bit reckless.

E. I live for drama.

F. I'd rather play or nap than do my homework.

6. How would your friends describe you?

A. I'm a total introvert.

B. I can be a bit of a grump.

C. I can be bribed with food.

D. I'm not afraid of anything.

E. I'm a trendsetter.

F. I make everyone laugh.

7. When you are upset, what helps you feel better?

A. A good cry.

B. Being left alone.

C. Ice cream—lots of it.

D. Exercise and getting fresh air.

E. Talking about what's bothering me with my friends.

F. Having fun and forgetting about it!

8. What is your best quality?

A. I'm a good friend.

B. I tell it like it is.

C. I'm always willing to share.

D. I'm brave.

E. Everyone likes me.

F. I'm always ready to have some fun.

Score Your Answers!

A=5 B=10 C=15 D=20 E=25 F=30

After scoring each answer, add up the total and write that number in the space below.

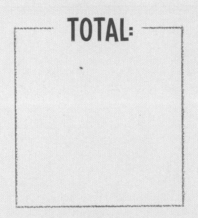

TOTAL:

Done adding up? Turn the page, look for your number, and find out what your cat personality is!

40–110: You are the **Cuddler!** You like to spend most of your day snuggled up somewhere comfy, and you are happiest when surrounded by those you love.

111–125: You are the **Couch Clawer!** You don't want to be poked, prodded, picked up, or petted. You like to be left alone and are sure to let people know when you're annoyed.

126–140: You are the **Food Lover!** You can often be found by your food bowl demanding second dinner. You're not mean about it, but you just want to make sure you get fed.

141–160: You are the **Curious Cat!** You have no fear. You'll climb the curtains and scale the highest shelf. The bigger the adventure, the more fun you have.

161–170: You are the **Influencer!** You're always rocking the latest fashions and accessories. You're no stranger to selfies, and you know how to get attention and have fun in the spotlight.

171–240: You are the **Playful Kitten!** When you're not napping, you're playing and chasing your tail. If it isn't fun, you don't want to do it!

Cat Tracker

Use this section to write about all the cats you meet, just like I do!

It's always fun to find a new feline friend. Use this Cat Tracker to document all the different cats you encounter, whether it's from a distance or up close and personal.

TUXEDO ○ Cat

Persian Cat

CAT in a SWEATER ○

Calico CAT ○

Tortoiseshell CAT ○

Scottish FOLD ○

BENGAL CAT ○

HIMALAYAN CAT ○

Hairless CAT ○

Siamese CAT ○

BLACK CAT ○

TABBY cat ○

Bookstore ○ CAT

Maine Coon ○

Cats to Look Out For

You never know when or where you'll see a cat, so keep an eye out! How many of these cats can you find?

☐ Bookstore cat

NAME: _____ DATE: _____

NOTES: _____

_____

☐ Cat on a leash

NAME: _____ DATE: _____

NOTES: _____

_____

☐ Cat in a sweater

NAME: _____ DATE: _____

NOTES: _____

_____

☐ Therapy cat

NAME: _____ DATE: _____

NOTES: _____

_____

☐ Hairless cat

NAME: _____ DATE: _____

NOTES: _____

_____

☐ Shorthaired cat

NAME: _____ DATE: _____

NOTES: _____

_____

☐ Longhaired cat

NAME: _____ DATE: _____

NOTES: _____

_____

☐ Polydactyl cat

NAME: _____ DATE: _____

NOTES: _____

_____

☐ Tabby cat

NAME: _____ DATE: _____

NOTES: _____

_____

☐ Black cat

NAME: _____ DATE: _____

NOTES: _____

_____

☐ Calico cat

NAME: _____ DATE: _____

NOTES: _____

_____

☐ Tuxedo cat

NAME: _____ DATE: _____

NOTES: _____

_____

☐ Tortoiseshell cat

NAME: _____ DATE: _____

NOTES: _____

_____

☐ Bodega cat

NAME: _____ DATE: _____

NOTES: _____

_____

Breeds

Here are some of the many cat breeds you may encounter. They each look a little different and will probably have very different personalities, too. How many have you spotted?

☐ **Abyssinian**

NAME: _____ DATE: _____

NOTES: _____

_____

☐ **American Bobtail**

NAME: _____ DATE: _____

NOTES: _____

_____

☐ **American Shorthair**

NAME: _____ DATE: _____

NOTES: _____

_____

☐ **American Wirehair**

NAME: _____ DATE: _____

NOTES: _____

_____

☐ Balinese

NAME: _____ DATE: _____

NOTES: _____

_____

☐ Bambino

NAME: _____ DATE: _____

NOTES: _____

_____

☐ Bengal

NAME: _____ DATE: _____

NOTES: _____

_____

☐ Birman

NAME: _____ DATE: _____

NOTES: _____

_____

☐ Bombay

NAME: _____ DATE: _____

NOTES: _____

_____

☐ British Shorthair

NAME: _____ DATE: _____

NOTES: _____

_____

☐ Burmese

NAME: _____ DATE: _____

NOTES: _____

_____

☐ Chartreux

NAME: _____ DATE: _____

NOTES: _____

_____

☐ Cornish Rex

NAME: _____ DATE: _____

NOTES: _____

_____

☐ Devon Rex

NAME: _____ DATE: _____

NOTES: _____

_____

☐ Egyptian Mau

NAME: _____ DATE: _____

NOTES: _____

_____

☐ Himalayan

NAME: _____ DATE: _____

NOTES: _____

_____

☐ Maine Coon

NAME: _____ DATE: _____

NOTES: _____

_____

☐ Manx

NAME: _____ DATE: _____

NOTES: _____

_____

☐ Munchkin

NAME: _____ DATE: _____

NOTES: _____

_____

☐ Norwegian Forest Cat

NAME: _____ DATE: _____

NOTES: _____

_____

☐ Ocicat

NAME: _____ DATE: _____

NOTES: _____

_____

☐ Persian

NAME: _____ DATE: _____

NOTES: _____

_____

☐ Ragamuffin

NAME: _____ DATE: _____

NOTES: _____

_____

☐ Ragdoll

NAME: _____ DATE: _____

NOTES: _____

_____

☐ Russian Blue

NAME: _____ DATE: _____

NOTES: _____

_____

☐ Scottish Fold

NAME: _____ DATE: _____

NOTES: _____

_____

☐ Siamese

NAME: _____ DATE: _____

NOTES: _____

_____

☐ Siberian

NAME: _____ DATE: _____

NOTES: _____

_____

☐ Somali

NAME: _____ DATE: _____

NOTES: _____

_____